MOTHER GOOSED

Nursery Rhymes for the Modern Woman

by Katherine Marris

Illustrations by Tim Williams

Published by Willis Harding, LLC
227 Sandy Springs Circle, Suite D-197
Sandy Springs, GA 30328
www.willisharding.com
www.katherinemarris.com

Printed in China

Mother Goosed, Nursery Rhymes for the Modern Woman / Katherine Marris.

FIRST EDITION, 2009

ISBN-13: 978-0-615-32254-4

FOR MOM AND DAD,
Roses are red, violets are blue,
my sweet Mo and Evelyn this one's for you.

You gave me a life that has perfect rhythm.

SPLAT

Little Miss Muffet
Sat on her tuffet,
Drinking her green herbal tea;
Along came a spider,
Thought he'd sit down beside her,
Thwack!! What a dead guy is he!

Mary had a little lamb,
She served it with green mint
and jam.

Do you know the muffin man
That lives in the top of my jeans?

It's raining, it's pouring,
PMS is roaring;
Get in bed, cover my head,
And don't get up til morning.

.12

Jack and Jill went up the hill,
Unfortunately, Jack left with Bill.

Big Boy Blue,
Don't blow your horn;
The red light was yellow,
Had to answer my phone.

Flash, flash I'm hot,
Sweat, sweat I'm cold;
Taking shots and gulping pills,
Darn, I'm getting old!

Shop a lot, shop a lot,
Banker man.
Make me a loan,
As fast as you can.

20

Jack be nimble,
Jack be quick,
I have a headache.

Twinkle, twinkle, little star,
Help me find where I parked my car.
Up above, or down below,
Back inside to shop I go.

Hey diddle, diddle!
What happened to the waist
'Round my middle?

Rub a dub, dub,
Wish I had a man in MY tub.

26

Hickory, dickory, dock!
There's an alarm on my biological clock.

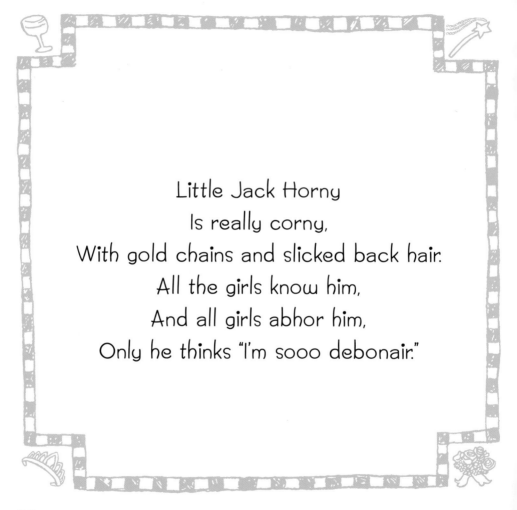

Little Jack Horny
Is really corny,
With gold chains and slicked back hair.
All the girls know him,
And all girls abhor him,
Only he thinks "I'm sooo debonair."

Mary, Mary quite contrary,
Oh, how your hormones rage!

Eeny, meeny, miny, moe,
Another bunion on my toe.

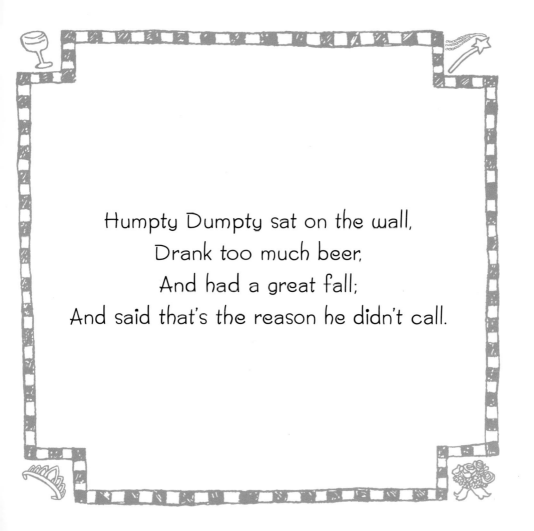

Humpty Dumpty sat on the wall,
Drank too much beer,
And had a great fall;
And said that's the reason he didn't call.

Georgie Porgie,
Puddin' and pie,
Kissed too many girls
And made me cry.

To market, to market,
To buy a fat hog;
That's how it feels,
When I go for a jog.

Hot cross bun,
My thong just snapped undone.

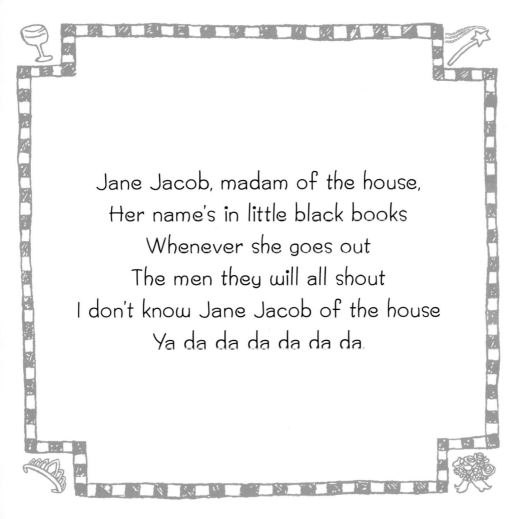

Jane Jacob, madam of the house,
Her name's in little black books
Whenever she goes out
The men they will all shout
I don't know Jane Jacob of the house
Ya da da da da da da.

One little, two little, three little sips of wine
Four little, five little, six more sips of wine,
Theven lithel, ate great big ole glugs,
Of glugs of the ole vino;
Oopsy, speeled nimber nine wine
Ten lissel
............zz zz z z z .

Little Bo Peep has lost her drive,
Can estrogen help her find it??

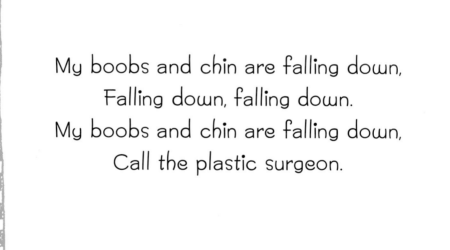

My boobs and chin are falling down,
Falling down, falling down.
My boobs and chin are falling down,
Call the plastic surgeon.

One, two,
buckle my shoe;
Three, four,
can't see the floor;
Five, six,
you need to get fixed;
Seven, eight,
no debate;
Nine, ten,
won't happen again!

Ring around the roses,
He finally proposes;
Champagne, champagne,
We all fall down.

Row, row, rows of gray
Growing on my head;
Some foils, some color and 2 hours later,
Back to golden red.

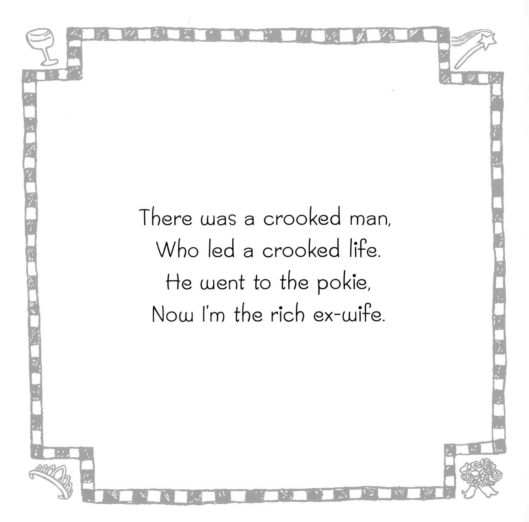

There was a crooked man,
Who led a crooked life.
He went to the pokie,
Now I'm the rich ex-wife.

Nouveau

Star light, star bright
To surgery I go tonight;
Roll me in, dim the light
Tuck my tummy good and tight.

There was a modern woman
Who lived in a shoe;
Lucky for her,
If they're Jimmy Choo.

This old man – he played two,
So I got the assets;
And all he got was you.

Middle, middle's plumping,
My diet's blown;
Went to bed with a triple dip cone.
One pound up, and one pound down;
Middle, middle's plumping,
My diet's blown.

The itsy bitsy lace bra,
It doesn't fit no more;
Three kids later,
They're closer to the floor.

All around the corporate world,
She chased the bucks and title;
'Til round her all the men fell down,
POP! she's in charge now!

TASTES
LIKE
CARDBOARD!

diet
cookie
bits

72

Old Mother Chubby
Went to the cubby,
To find a midnight snack;
When she got there
The cubby was bare,
Except for that dumb diet pack.

Here is the church
Guests fill the room,
Open the door
...uh oh, no groom??

Sing a song of diamonds,
Perfect clarity.
4 and 20 facets,
No irregularity.
When the box is opened,
She begins to sing;
Isn't that the perfect stone,
To set upon my ring?

Dark, Dark chocolate, have PMS,
Ate it, ate it, what a mess.
Sauce on my ice cream,
Icing on my cake,
And chips in the cookies I didn't even bake.

A Pucci, a Gucci,
Some green and yellow sushi;
A great big bill, dressed to kill,
And on the front I dripped it.

I rubbed it, I rubbed it,
And on the front I scrubbed it;
Add the tag, back in the bag,
Back to the store I schlepped it.

Pain, pain is on the way,
Mother-in-law coming to stay;
The wretched woman is her own cliché,
Pain, pain go away.

This little chicky went to Neiman's,
This little chicky shopped from home;
This little chicky looked for bargains,
This little chicky found none;
This little chicky cried
charge, charge, charge,
all the way home.

Hair, eyebrows, nails, and toes,
Nails and toes,
Foils, Facial, fix my nose,
Fix my nose.

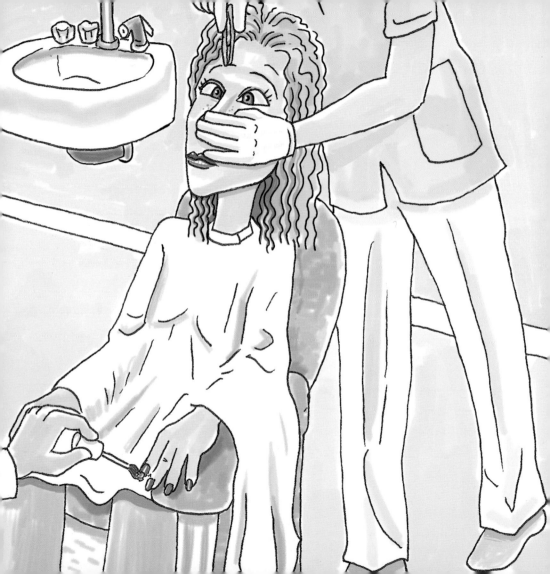

Monday's girl is tired from fun,
Tuesday's girl is on the run,
Wednesday's girl is over the hump,
Thursday's girl is in a slump,
Friday's Girl is ready to go,
Saturday's girl is out for show,
But Sunday's girl is a real grouch
With sweats, and pets, she's on the couch.

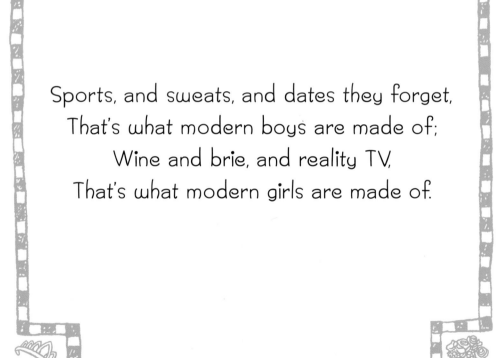

Sports, and sweats, and dates they forget,
That's what modern boys are made of;
Wine and brie, and reality TV,
That's what modern girls are made of.

Fee, fie, flow, foam
Triple, grand latte
Before I leave home!

This is the house that Kat built.
This is the malt that lay 'round
the house that Kat built.
This is the rat that drank the malt
That lay round the house that Kat built.
This is the Kat that threw out the rat
That drank the malt
that lay 'round the house
that Kat built.

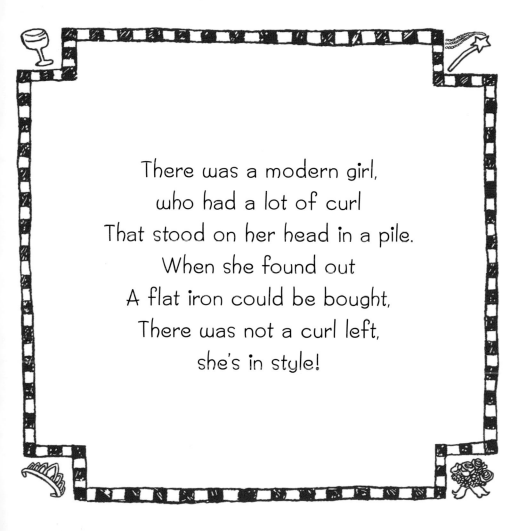

There was a modern girl,
who had a lot of curl
That stood on her head in a pile.
When she found out
A flat iron could be bought,
There was not a curl left,
she's in style!

Three old kittens have rusty fittin's,
Never know how long they'll last;
When they giggle, they start to wiggle,
And run to the girl's room fast!

100

Rock n' Roll baby,
How you've grown up;
Leather and fringes,
No more your cup;

Piercings and tattoos,
Now just old scars;
No more cheap wine, eight tracks,
or electric guitars.

Three blind dates,
Three Blind dates,
See how I run!
See how I run!
They all posted pictures on catch.com,
But one was balding and one was dumb.
I think they should call it batch o' dot bums,
No more blind dates.

Queen mom with a heart
Wanted to do her part,
And bake for the PTA;
The first batch she burned
On the second she learned,
It's easier just to pay.

ABOUT THE AUTHOR

Once upon a time, (longer than she's willing to admit), and not so very far away, there lived a little girl with red hair and freckles that loved to create. She loved to climb trees and read books and dream about being the character in a book. She wrote little stories and turned them into books written on three ring notebook paper.

As the little girl grew she loved to design and sew, fire pottery, paint, do needlework and generally create beauty from anything she could find.

Then the girl became a woman and put all that aside to learn how to color inside the lines where creativity is appreciated only as it translates into corporate profit. In this forest, she lost her sense of adventure, her "*Jiminy*", the ability to slow down, ponder, wish upon a star. And as a wise cricket once said, "Let your conscience be your guide." But, there is a happy ending to this girl's story. In each life story rhythms change and this big girl found the trail of bread crumbs left behind. Stale as they were, she changed the borders, got out the crayons and started thinking outside the margin again, recreating her life.

There are lessons in fairy tales. The moral to this girl's story is this: the worst of times are tough, but they can and should be a very real investment on the road to the best of times that can come if you reach back inside and find what you love to do. You'll get your *Jiminy* back!

Katherine Marris has lived in the Atlanta area for over 30 years, a single mom to two kids, and Mimi to a fabulous granddaughter.

OTHER INSPIRATIONS
by Katherine Marris

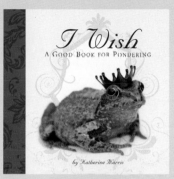

A GOOD BOOK FOR PONDERING

124 full color pages of wishes that will make you smile, laugh out loud,
shed a few tears and think about what you really wish.
A perfect gift for anyone at any age, this little book is full of wisdom and humor.
Available at www.willisharding.com or check out our list of retailers
on the website for the store nearest you.

To learn about the author go to her blog at katherinemarris.com.
Katherine is available for book signings, speeches and appearances
because they're a lot of fun!

THE END
Live Happily Ever After